AF434582

Foreword

We have always lived with a certain amount of uncertainty. Life is a series of choices and in every choice there is an element of risk that we must adopt. We can meticulously plan for the future but nothing is 100% guaranteed.

With the universal potential exposure to COVID-19, we now have been thrown into a sense of awareness that we are not invincible and that each moment we have is a gift and is precious.

"In the Light of Uncertainty" encourages each individual to take this challenging time as a pause in everyday life to evaluate and reinvent yourself.

Sometimes that means appreciating the people that love you, seeing love in others or embracing love for yourself.

We all need encouragement right now but know with every day that passes, you will get stronger and wiser and more creative.

My hope is by reading these series of poems, you will feel motivated to accept the current circumstance, embrace your beautiful self and find your happiness within.

Much love,

Isabella Evangeline

Dedicated
to
those
who just
sometimes
need a friend
who will
listen intently
for just a moment…

40 days &

40 nights...

Are you being tested?

blink

I saw laughter
Tasted freedom
Feasted on joy
My soul
full of
Love.

Then I blinked...
And
Everything changed.
Darkness unfolded
Fear emerged.
So I grasped onto
Hope
Took shelter
in suffering
Cherished
All that I had
As gratefulness
took my hand.

Uncertainty

Trapped in a maze
without control
Frozen in place
But running inside.
An unbelievable puzzle
i'm getting dizzy
Trying to figure it out…

        The outcome
        The solution.

Where do I step?
How far will it go?
To survive
I must embrace
this feeling
and make it my friend.

War

We are at war
with the great Unknown.
Fear rises
as levels of
Uncertainty form.
What are you made of
What will you do
When faced
With a challenge
So insurmountable
So fierce.
Brainstorm
or
Storm the brain.
Trivial pursuits
are long forgotten
and the simple joys
Remain
Sanitizing
Reshaping
our souls from
the inner core.

the fog

Traversing through life
Carefully planting
our feet
Strategically.
         Specific calculations
         Cautious measures.
Abruptly
         It rolls in
Threatening
to consume
All.

Still
Beauty
will be found
in-between the chaos.

the Catalyst

Innocently comfortable
But deep inside
something was stirring
Brewing
Trying
to grab her attention
                 noticed only
                           in times of
                                   Stillness.

And then it happened
so much destruction
Chaos
Motivating her
to create
a new path
Not originally
intended.
Like dominos
         Her story unfolded
                  Giving her
                      A fantastic new beginning.

We are

our most creative

when we are pushed

against a wall

with nothing to lose.

Panicked

My heart
was exploding
My head
was racing
My body
on fire
My hands
were shaking.
My mind
Confused
i couldn't stop
crying
i never felt
so weak.
Was this it?
Was I dying?

Then it stopped
As suddenly
As it started
It seemed like a test
to get my attention.
But really
it humbled me
made me
So grateful
to be
Alive.

Adversity

Pushed
Pulled
on all sides
I must face it
Head on
Stand tall
Proud.
Bundled in
Love
Wrapped tight
in confidence
Gripping hard
to that courage
to endure
this perfect storm
Only to strengthen
Layer me
with Resilience
deep within.

the Shield

An unknown battle
scarce resources
Impending doom
Terrifying all.
But one element
Protects
Cures
is the root
of a remedy
The hope
of a solution.
You don't have to
wait for it
You already have
Plenty.
Hold tightly
and use it
in abundance

Love.

Up side of down

I lifted myself
High into the clouds
Not a soul in sight
as loneliness set in.
Disillusioned
I lost my footing
Fell
Twisting
Spiraling
      Down
         So
           fast
vulnerable
Grateful for
Your outstretched hand.

survive or Thrive

In the midst of uproar
Overshadowed by fear
Our mortality
at risk
The first thought
Is…
Survive.
The basic needs
Become our
Only
Desire.
But after the shock
Embrace   heights.
this opportunity   new
To break the mold   to
                    And soar

Your use of words

hold much **POWER**.

The first step

Take a step
Toward

Away
from the past.
It's heavy and scary
but the aftermath is
Change.
It doesn't matter
what happened
Yesterday.

Now is the time
to try something new.
Right now
You can become
the person you desire
Despite
your
previous
Choices.

Coaching the mind

Say less
Relish the experience
Don't overthink
Let things fall in place.
Don't be demanding or pushy.
Be the best version of
Yourself.
Listen
Observe
Speak what you mean
Take your time
Don't rush
Be loving
Be kind
But know when to
remove yourself
from a toxic environment
And focus
on other things
that are
the most important to
You.

A sharpening of senses

I've noticed things
I've never noticed before.
Kind neighbors
exchanging a laugh.
A stranger's smile
from across the street.
The bird sitting
at the top
of the tallest tree.
A butterfly
Leading me
along its journey.
Encouraging words
written
on a sidewalk.
Take someone
out of their
normal routine
And they see
the world
As it is.

stripped

Vanity
is peeled off
layer by layer
to reveal the
authenticity
of self.
Priorities change
Things that were given
so much time
Effort
are now
irrelevant.
Dive into the interior
clean out the
Societal infection
causing so much chaos
and pain
to quench
a much-needed thirst
for aspiration
and purpose.

Last words

Don't wait
till the end
to say
what
you need
to say
Say it now.

Love
like you've
never loved.
Live
Learn
Dream
Create
Don't procrastinate
Do it
     right now.

It's easy to be critical

But people just want to be **Seen**.

Observing the perception

Next time
you want to judge
Give your opinion
Present your view
Ask yourself...
Is this an observation
backed up by facts
concrete Truth.
Or is it my perception
My truth
Shadowing all
Filling my head
Colored by my experience
and circumstance.

The struggle to be Understood

Everyday
I view myself
in looking out.
Smiling to be kind
interpreted as interest.
My professionalism is seen
as indifference.
Caring and asking questions
Comes off as intrusive.
My passion
Is deemed aggressive.
I am vulnerable
Yet you see me as
Too emotional.

So all in all
I found
the only one
who will

                   completely
                   Understand you

Is
YOU.

my house

Come on in…
I've got so much
to tell.
Each room
has a past
a story
so colorful.
Stay here
awhile.
It is safe.
Each window
is a mirror
of unlocked secrets.
Let's laugh
and cry
and share
this space.
The door
      is always
         open
           to
            You.

genuine

Tell me your story
from the very beginning
Your happiest times
Your greatest fears
Your hopes
and wildest dreams.
I want to know
Every time your heart
was broken.
Every person
You've loved
and why.
Your deepest regrets
Your weaknesses
Your successes
'cause you're so genuine
to me.

ingredients of self

We have the ability
to choose
from the array of elements
Factors
placed around us.
Will you reach for
A bit of love
A pinch of compassion
or a splash of hate?
Mix peace with joy
to create a unique
recipe for
Deeply fulfilled
or select envy
seasoned with bitterness
to ingest a concoction
Only to poison ourselves.

Are you the person
                inside looking out
                        or the person

Observed by others?

secrets revealed

If we had
All the answers
There would be no
Struggle
No hard-earned discoveries
No character built
No strengthening
of heart
mind
and soul.
We would be
lifeless
just laying there
with no purpose
No reason
Motivation
to do anything
More.
Secrets exist
To spur us on
To give us a cause
A choice
To become
      who we want
To become.

karma

It's not about
being nice
so that
good things
come back
to you.

It's about
putting your
beautiful imprint
on the world.
Your strengths
Your talents
Your wisdom
giving back
to make
our world
a better place.

the hidden door

She was limited
to the room.
At first glance
Everything was familiar
Mundane.
But her senses
Slowly awakened
Intensified by
Silence
and the need
for a decision
to be made.
And this spun her
to find
the hidden door.

As it was opened
So was her heart.

glimpse

The darker it becomes
the brighter you shine.
As the pollution
infiltrates
You fight to stay clean.
It is gloomier
But you are happier.
The present situation is heavier
yet you feel lighter.
It was that
glimpse
of missing the future
that made you
Grateful
for today.

Explosion

The façade is gone
Whoever you thought
you were
you're not.

Instead
i see you.
Bare
without
Superficiality
With
a new humility
The real you
is shining
through

            Illuminating
            All.

Create your own song

      you sing everyday...

Many paths to Happiness

One was young
One was foolish
One was obedient
One lacked judgment.

The youth succeeded
in every aspect
Then lost his wealth
But found himself.

Everything the fool touched
turned to darkness
But he made the choice
to change his ways.

The obedient one
was unhappy most of his life
Until he decided
to do what he loved.

And the one
who lacked judgment
Finally made a decision
that turned his life
Completely around.

the Bridge

Climbing the mountain
the journey is hard
Tough
We struggle to keep moving
Don't stop for diversions
Temptations
Leading us
Astray.
When we reach
The top
The sacrifice is worth it.
The steep ascension
worth the stunning view.
And when you see
Another magnificent peak
Keep going
Don't   and go up   But build__a__bridge.
    descend

The strength of Awareness

They say
ignorance is bliss
But I say
a taste of wisdom
Understanding
is more sensational
than anything.
So much knowledge
Exists
waiting
to be found.

When they say
you think too much
I say you think
too little.
From awareness
comes Wisdom
Silent
Yet satisfying.
Learning from your
surroundings
tuning into
reality
Finding
Hidden truths
and meaning.

The road less travelled

Several paths
to choose from
Most will walk
the paved one
with few bumps
and more guarantees.

I chose
a different one
off to the side
It was bumpy
Risky
I was curious
It was adventurous
and more
Rewarding
than
I could have
Ever
Imagined.

the crab

It was far
in the distance
then edged closer
A tremendous wave
Unexpected
Threatening to overtake
Engulf
Everything.
Most would panic
yet the crab saw its
Timely opportunity
Planned
and was
Calm
Resilient
Adaptable
Brilliant
to escape
through the tiny crevice
below.

It is more rewarding

To love

than be

loved.

The Power of Love

The old man
had always
suffered
greatly.
He had never
found love
But heartache
and pain.
He had no family
left.
Lived a life
of poverty.
Struggled
Endlessly
to get up
each day.

And then
> She smiled at him
> And it all
> Changed.

Transformation

It was time.
He had worn
the mask
for too long.
Deteriorating
about to reveal
Secret burdens
Mysterious ways.
Take it off
Find comfort
in vulnerability.
As you look
in the mirror
See yourself
Evolve
Transform.

the meeting of YOUs

Walking along
Traveling down
the complexity of
My path
I came across
a circle
of Yous
Huddled
they were arguing
Different ages
Different stages
of your life.
They didn't get along
Couldn't see eye to eye
Too busy to notice
I joined.

The island

There you were
My paradise
But I rushed past you
i didn't notice you
or stop to explore.
I was lost in the thrill
of temporary
Distractions
Alluring destinations
Unable
to discover
Your hidden treasures
Your sustainability
Your bliss.

Vipassana

Sheltered in place
isolated from all
With the choice
to talk
or be silent.
With the choice
to walk
or be still.
Worries released
Loosened control
The mind is the body
The body is the mind.
A fresh outlook
A blank slate
to create a life
of my choice
As
I see things
As
they truly are.

In the midst of loving yourself,

you see LOVE all around you…

Revolution

It's coming
We are rising
Above
Acceptable norms
Questioning
Everything.
A new wave of ideas
Combining
Creative minds
throughout
our redefined world.
We have been
Awakened.
Get out of your
Comfort zone
and join the fight
for our future.

Empowered

Do you feel
that electricity
Flowing through
Your veins
Your uniqueness
Leading you
to something great.
On the brink of
New discoveries
New ideas
Taking your mind
to new places
Tapping into a
Strength you've always
Had
But needed to find
Inside.

Freedom

It's when
you tell the truth
when everyone
expects you to lie.
It's sticking to your
Beliefs
when others think
you're foolish.
It's dancing away
a particularly hard day.
It's loving others
not caring if
they love you back.
It's being destitute
But so grateful
and happy
for anything at all.
It's having the courage
to be yourself
at all costs.
It's not caring
what people think
But being happy
with who you
Truly
Are.

a joyful life

Every minute
I'm in tune
to the joy
of each task.
Individual moments
adding up
to an incredible day.
That first sip
of coffee.
The acceptance
of meditation.
The healing warmth
of the sun.
The soothing sound
of rain.
The radiant cheer
of birds singing.
The satisfaction
of finishing
a tough project.
Taking care
of my home
as an extension of myself.
Dancing unapologetically
in the shower.
The hidden strength
of yoga.
With each enjoyment
comes much reward
I couldn't ask
for anything more.

Embracing the Unknown

Life is uncertain
You're not promised
tomorrow
Empower
Yourself
Today.
Set lofty goals
Watch
as you soar
to incredible new heights.
Remember
as you step up
to fear
It becomes smaller
as you become
Stronger.
Cherish
what you have
Enjoy
those precious moments
Take account
of your blessings
Change
what doesn't bring
Happiness.
Be responsible
But live each day
to the absolute fullest.

Acknowledgments

So many times we dream about being at a certain place in life. What we don't understand, is that the real treasure and reward is the journey itself.

This pandemic has allowed and gifted me with the opportunity to really re-evaluate myself. It has thrown me into a rollercoaster of emotions, from being absolutely terrified to deeply examining myself internally to feeling empowered that I have control of my actions and reactions despite my environment and the changing world around me.

Thank you to all that have been sacrificial in the light of uncertainty today:

Mothers, fathers, healthcare workers, biotech companies, delivery drivers, grocery workers, postal workers, first responders, essential business workers, friends appreciating and encouraging friends, strangers looking out for strangers...You are all so deeply appreciated and loved by so many!!!!